Our
Noodles & Rice Recipes

Copyright 2010, Gooseberry Patch
Second Printing, November, 2010

A range of cooking times is often given on packages of pasta.
The first cooking time is for al dente (firm to the bite) and the
second cooking time is for a softer pasta. You choose!

Hamburger Heaven

Serves 4

1 lb. ground beef
8-oz. pkg. American cheese
   slices
1 c. celery, chopped
2-1/4 oz. can sliced black
   olives, drained

2 c. fine egg noodles, uncooked
14-1/2 oz. can stewed tomatoes
1/2 c. water

Brown beef in a large skillet over medium heat; drain and return to skillet. Layer remaining ingredients except water over beef in order given. Pour water over all. Cover; simmer for 30 minutes, or until noodles are tender.

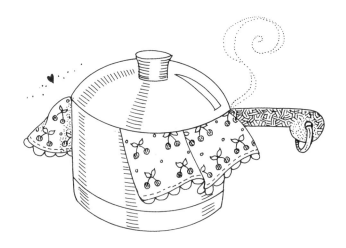

The secret to tender steamed rice! Cook long-cooking rice according to package directions. When it's done, remove pan from heat, cover with a folded tea towel and put lid back on. Let stand for 5 to 10 minutes before serving.

Chicken & Wild Rice

Serves 4

1/2 lb. sliced mushrooms
2 T. butter
2 c. cooked chicken, diced
6-oz. pkg. long-grain and wild
   rice mix, cooked

1/2 c. sour cream
10-3/4 oz. can cream of
   mushroom soup

In a saucepan over medium heat, sauté mushrooms in butter until tender. Add remaining ingredients. Mix gently; spread in a lightly greased 2-quart casserole dish. Bake, uncovered, at 350 degrees for 30 minutes, until heated through.

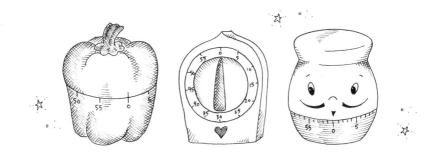

Save time and money with family-size packages of ground beef.
Place beef in a stockpot, add a little water to prevent sticking and
cook over medium-high heat until browned, stirring often.
Drain well and pack recipe-size portions in freezer bags.

Paula's Baked Ziti

Serves 6

1 lb. ground beef, browned
    and drained
4 c. ziti pasta, cooked
28-oz. jar spaghetti sauce

1 c. grated Parmesan-Romano
    cheese, divided
8-oz. pkg. shredded mozzarella
    cheese

Combine beef, ziti, sauce and 3/4 cup grated cheese in a large
bowl; mix well. Spread in a lightly greased 13"x9" baking pan;
sprinkle with mozzarella cheese. Bake, uncovered, at 375 degrees
for about 20 minutes, until hot and bubbly. Garnish with remaining
grated cheese.

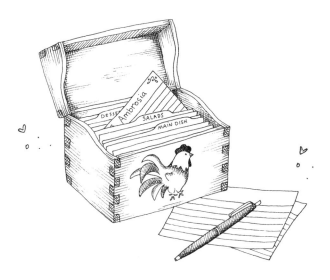

Make up some handy file cards listing the ingredients needed
for your most-used dinner recipes...shopping will be a breeze!

Chicken & Sausage Supreme

Serves 4 to 6

4 to 6 chicken breasts, cooked and cubed
1 lb. ground pork sausage, browned and drained
5-oz. pkg. yellow rice, cooked
10-3/4 oz. can cream of chicken soup

In a large bowl, combine chicken and sausage. Add rice and stir well; blend in soup. Spoon into a lightly greased 13"x9" baking pan. Bake, uncovered, at 350 degrees for 20 to 30 minutes, or until golden and heated through.

For baked casseroles, cook pasta for the shortest cooking time
recommended on the package. It's not necessary to rinse
the cooked pasta, just drain it well.

Quick & Easy Lasagna

Makes 12 servings

1 lb. ground beef, browned
3 16-oz. cans tomato sauce
16-oz. pkg. lasagna noodles,
    cooked and divided

2 c. cottage cheese, divided
16-oz. pkg. shredded
    mozzarella cheese, divided

Mix ground beef and tomato sauce together; set aside. Spread 1/4 cup tomato sauce mixture in the bottom of a greased 13"x9" baking pan; layer with about half the noodles. Pour half the sauce mixture on top; drop half the cottage cheese by spoonfuls into the sauce mixture. Sprinkle with half the mozzarella cheese; repeat layers beginning with noodles. Bake, uncovered, at 350 degrees until cheese melts, about 20 to 25 minutes.

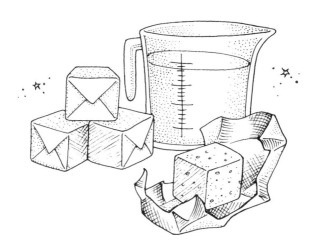

Here's an easy, thrifty way to give pasta or rice lots more flavor... just toss a bouillon cube or two into the cooking water.

Skillet Turkey Stroganoff

Serves 4

1 lb. ground turkey, browned
    and drained
10-3/4 oz. can cream of
    mushroom soup

1 c. sour cream
1/2 c. milk
cooked whole-wheat egg
    noodles

Combine all ingredients except noodles in a skillet over medium heat. Cook until thickened, stirring occasionally, about 15 minutes. Serve spooned over cooked noodles.

It's always best to fluff rice with a fork after cooking
instead of stirring with a spoon...with a fork
it's sure to be fluffy every time!

Pepper Steak

Serves 4 to 6

2 T. cornstarch
1-1/2 c. plus 2 T. water, divided
3 T. oil, divided
1 T. soy sauce
1/8 t. pepper

1 lb. beef round steak or sirloin,
  cut into strips
2 green peppers, cut into strips
2 T. garlic, pressed
1-1/2 c. cooked rice

Combine cornstarch, 2 tablespoons water, one tablespoon oil, soy sauce and pepper in a bowl; stir in beef strips and set aside. Heat one tablespoon oil in a wok or large skillet; sauté green peppers over medium heat until crisp-tender. Remove peppers from skillet; set aside. Add remaining oil to skillet; add garlic and sauté until golden. Add beef mixture to skillet; cook for one minute without stirring. Cook and stir until meat is cooked medium-rare; remove from skillet. Add remaining water; bring to a boil. Remove from heat and stir in cooked rice. Top with beef and peppers; cover and let stand for at least 5 minutes before serving.

Better than a feast elsewhere is a meal at home of tea and rice.

~Japanese proverb

Spicy Pork Noodle Bowls

Serves 4

8-oz. pkg. linguine pasta,
    uncooked
2 T. oil, divided
1 lb. boneless pork shoulder,
    sliced into strips
1 onion, thinly sliced
1/2 lb. broccoli, cut into
    bite-size flowerets

2 T. Worcestershire sauce
1 T. soy sauce
2 t. cornstarch
1/2 t. curry powder
1 tomato, chopped

Cook half of pasta according to package directions; set aside. Reserve remaining pasta for another recipe. Heat one tablespoon oil in a large skillet over high heat. Add pork; cook and stir until golden, about 7 minutes. Remove pork; set aside. Heat remaining oil in skillet; add onion and broccoli. Cook and stir until tender, about 5 minutes. Mix together sauces, cornstarch and curry powder in a cup; stir into skillet. Cook and stir until slightly thickened. Return pork to pan; heat through. Divide cooked pasta into 4 shallow bowls. Top with pork mixture and tomato; toss to coat pasta.

Traditionally made with cold cooked rice, fried rice is
a super way to turn all kinds of leftover cooked meat and
veggies into a family-pleasing meal. Check the fridge,
then mix & match as you like!

Aunt Marcie's Fried Rice

Makes 8 to 10 servings

1/2 lb. bacon, crisply cooked
    and crumbled,
      5 T. drippings reserved
6 eggs, beaten
1/4 t. salt

3 c. cooked rice, chilled
3/4 c. frozen peas, thawed
1 T. soy sauce
2 T. green onion, sliced

In a large skillet, heat 3 tablespoons reserved drippings until very hot. Beat eggs and salt together with a fork; pour egg mixture into skillet. Cook, stirring quickly and constantly with a spoon until eggs are the size of peas. Reduce heat to low; push eggs to one side of skillet. In same skillet, gently stir rice and remaining drippings until rice is well coated. Add bacon, peas and soy sauce. Gently stir to mix; heat through. Spoon into a serving bowl and sprinkle with green onion.

Chicken thighs are extra flavorful, juicy and easy on the budget, but are usually sold with the bone in. To speed up cooking time, use a sharp knife to make a deep cut on each side of the bone.

Chicken & Onions over Pasta   *Makes 6 to 8 servings*

2 T. oil
6 to 8 boneless, skinless
    chicken thighs
1 to 2 t. garlic powder
1 t. pepper
2 onions, sliced
3 to 4 c. water

6 cubes beef bouillon
1 t. dried oregano
8-oz. pkg. linguine pasta,
    cooked
Garnish: grated Parmesan
    cheese

Heat oil over medium heat in a large pot; add chicken and sauté until golden, about 15 to 20 minutes. Sprinkle chicken with garlic powder and pepper. Add onions to pot; sauté for 2 minutes. Add water to cover chicken; stir in bouillon cubes and oregano. Bring to a boil; lower heat, cover and simmer for 20 minutes. Uncover and simmer an additional 10 minutes. To serve, place cooked pasta in a deep serving bowl; pour chicken mixture over pasta. Let stand several minutes. Sprinkle with Parmesan cheese.

For juicy, tender chicken in recipes calling for cooked chicken,
try poaching. Cover boneless, skinless chicken breasts with water
in a saucepan. Bring to a boil, then turn down the heat, cover and
simmer over low heat for 10 to 12 minutes. The chicken is
done when it is no longer pink in the center.

Baked Chicken Washington

Makes 3 to 4 servings

1/4 c. all-purpose flour
1 T. chicken bouillon granules
1/4 c. butter, melted
2 c. milk
3 c. cooked chicken, cubed
4-oz. jar sliced mushrooms,
    drained

1/4 c. green pepper, chopped
2 T. pimento
1-1/2 c. long-cooking rice,
    cooked
1 c. shredded Swiss cheese

Blend flour and bouillon into butter in a saucepan over medium heat.
Add milk; cook until thickened. Remove from heat and fold in
chicken, mushrooms, pepper and pimento. Spread rice in a buttered
8"x8" casserole dish. Top with chicken mixture; sprinkle with cheese.
Bake, uncovered, at 350 degrees for 30 minutes.

A quick & easy seasoning mix is six parts salt to one part pepper.
Keep it close to the stove in a large shaker...so handy when
pan-frying pork chops or chicken.

Pork Chops Olé

Serves 4 to 6

2 T. olive oil
6 pork chops, cut 1/2-inch thick
seasoned salt and pepper
  to taste
3/4 c. long-cooking rice,
  uncooked

1-1/2 c. water
8-oz. can tomato sauce
2 T. taco seasoning mix
1 green pepper, chopped
1 c. shredded Cheddar cheese

Heat oil in a large skillet over medium heat; add pork chops and brown on both sides. Sprinkle with salt and pepper; set aside. Combine rice, water, tomato sauce and taco seasoning; mix well. Pour into a lightly greased 13"x9" baking pan; arrange pork chops on top of rice mixture. Sprinkle with green pepper; cover and bake at 350 degrees for 30 to 45 minutes. Uncover; sprinkle with cheese. Return to oven and bake until cheese melts, about 5 minutes.

Cooking up an extra-quick spaghetti dinner?
Choose angel hair pasta...it takes just three minutes
to cook, once the water is boiling.

Grandma Goldie's Sketti

Serves 4

8-oz. pkg. pasteurized process
   cheese spread, cubed
2 c. stewed tomatoes in juice
1 to 2 T. sugar

1/4 t. celery seed
salt and pepper to taste
8-oz. pkg. spaghetti, cooked

Combine all ingredients except spaghetti in a medium saucepan. Cook over low heat until cheese is almost melted, stirring constantly to prevent scorching. Use a wooden spoon to mash up tomatoes well. Remove from heat; toss in spaghetti and stir to coat well. Transfer to a serving bowl.

If a recipe calls for canned tomatoes, take advantage of
Mexican or Italian-style. They already have the seasonings
added, so there are fewer ingredients for you
to buy and measure!

Spanish Rice

Serves 6

1-1/2 lbs. ground beef
2 10-3/4 oz. cans tomato soup
1/4 c. green pepper, chopped

Optional: 1/4 c. onion, chopped
1-1/2 c. instant rice, cooked

Brown ground beef in a large skillet over medium heat; drain. Add tomato soup, green pepper and onion, if using; mix well. Add rice, stirring gently. Simmer for 15 minutes.

Homemade chicken broth is simple to make. Whenever you
boil chicken for a recipe, save the cooking liquid and freeze it.
When it's time to make broth, thaw and combine with desired
amount of chopped onion, carrots and celery. Simmer, uncovered,
one hour and strain if desired.

One-Pot Chicken & Noodles

Serves 6

26-oz. can cream of chicken
    soup
10-3/4 oz. can cream of
    mushroom soup
3 14-1/2 oz. cans chicken
    broth
2 c. cooked chicken breast,
    diced

2 t. onion powder
1 t. seasoning salt
1/2 t. garlic powder
2 9-oz. pkgs. frozen wide
    egg noodles, uncooked

Combine soups, broth and chicken in a large pot; bring to a boil over
medium-high heat. Add remaining ingredients; reduce heat to low
and simmer for 20 to 30 minutes, until noodles are tender.

For another way to enjoy Mexican Chicken Olé, spoon into warm flour tortillas. Top with sour cream, guacamole and salsa to taste. Roll up and serve...delicious!

Mexican Chicken Olé

Serves 4

1 T. olive oil
4 boneless, skinless chicken
    breasts
salt and pepper to taste
15-1/4 oz. can corn, drained
15-oz. can black beans, drained
    and rinsed

14-1/2 oz. can diced tomatoes
    with chiles
1 c. shredded Cheddar cheese
cooked yellow rice

Heat oil in a frying pan over medium heat. Add chicken breasts;
sprinkle with salt and pepper to taste. Brown chicken for 3 to
4 minutes on each side. Top chicken with corn, black beans and
tomatoes with chiles; do not stir. Cover pan and cook over medium-
low heat for 15 to 20 minutes. Uncover; top with cheese. Turn heat
to low and cook for an additional 5 minutes, until cheese melts.
Serve with cooked rice.

Frozen veggies come in so many colorful, delicious blends...
and they're almost as good as homegrown. Add variety
to favorite recipes or toss with dried herbs and
crispy bacon for a quick side.

Bowtie Pasta & Veggies

Serves 4 to 6

2 T. oil
16-oz. pkg. frozen mixed
    vegetables, thawed
1 yellow squash, diced
1 zucchini, diced
8-oz. pkg. bowtie pasta, cooked
1/4 t. garlic, minced

1/2 t. salt
1/2 c. shredded mozzarella
    cheese
1/2 c. shredded provolone
    cheese
1/2 c. shredded Parmesan
    cheese

Heat oil in a large saucepan over medium heat; sauté vegetables together until lightly golden and tender. Stir in cooked pasta, garlic and salt. Sprinkle with cheeses and stir until melted.

Cook a double batch of rice, then freeze half in a plastic freezer bag for another meal. When you're ready to use the frozen rice, just microwave on high for one minute per cup to thaw, 2 to 3 minutes per cup to warm it through. Fluff with a fork...ready to use!

Beefy Rice Bake

1 lb. ground beef
1 c. instant rice, cooked
14-1/2 oz. can diced tomatoes
4-oz. can sliced mushrooms,
    drained

10-3/4 oz. can cream of
    mushroom soup
1 T. Cajun seasoning
8-oz. pkg. shredded sharp
    Cheddar cheese

Brown ground beef in a large skillet over medium heat; drain. Add rice, tomatoes, mushrooms, soup and seasoning; mix well. Cook for 5 minutes, or until heated through. Spread mixture in a lightly greased 13"x9" baking pan. Sprinkle with cheese. Bake, uncovered, at 350 degrees for 10 minutes, or until cheese is melted.

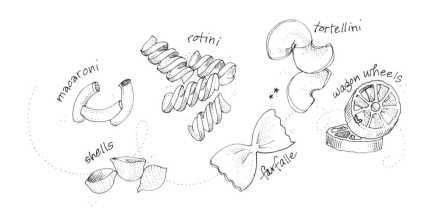

macaroni

rotini

tortellini

wagon wheels

shells

farfalle

Mix up a favorite macaroni recipe by substituting different
types of pasta. Check out the pasta aisle for bowties,
rotini, wagon wheels or shells.

Cheesy Macaroni Skillet

Serves 4

2 c. elbow macaroni, uncooked
1/2 lb. bacon, diced
14-1/2 oz. can diced tomatoes

8-oz. can tomato sauce
1 c. shredded Cheddar cheese

Cook macaroni according to package directions; drain. Fry bacon in a large skillet until crisp. Drain, leaving about one tablespoon drippings in skillet. Add tomatoes with juice, tomato sauce and cooked macaroni. Simmer over low heat until hot and bubbly, about 20 minutes. Add cheese; place lid on skillet and let stand until cheese is melted, about 5 minutes.

Make a fresh-tasting side dish in a jiffy. Combine 3 to 4 sliced zucchini, 1/2 teaspoon minced garlic and a tablespoon of chopped fresh basil. Sauté in a little olive oil until tender.

Herbed Chicken & Rice Bake

Serves 4 to 6

3 to 4 lbs. chicken
1 c. long-cooking rice,
    uncooked
2 10-3/4 oz. cans cream of
    chicken soup

1-1/4 c. water
1-1/2 oz. pkg. onion soup mix
1 t. dried thyme
1 t. Worcestershire sauce

Arrange chicken pieces in a lightly greased deep 13"x9" baking pan;
set aside. Stir together remaining ingredients; spread evenly over
chicken. Cover tightly with aluminum foil. Bake at 350 degrees
for 2-1/2 hours, until rice is tender and chicken juices run clear
when pierced.

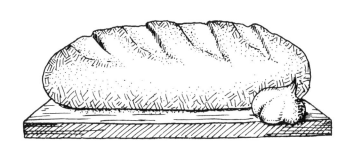

For an easy beginning to a savory meal, set out a piping-hot loaf
of Italian bread and a little dish of olive oil sprinkled
with Italian seasoning for dipping.

Chicken & Sausage Skilletini

Serves 4 to 6

2 T. olive oil
2 boneless, skinless chicken
    breasts, cubed
1/2 lb. spicy ground pork
    sausage
1 red onion, thinly sliced
2 cloves garlic, minced
1 red pepper, sliced

14-1/2 oz. can diced tomatoes
3 T. brown sugar, packed
1/2 t. dried oregano
1 t. dried basil
1/8 t. salt
1/8 t. pepper
16-oz. pkg. linguine pasta,
    cooked

Heat oil in a large skillet over medium heat. Add chicken, sausage, onion, garlic and pepper; cook until chicken and sausage are cooked through. Drain. Add remaining ingredients except pasta; simmer for 5 minutes. Add cooked pasta to skillet; simmer for an additional 5 minutes.

Freeze leftover cooked rice for quick-fix meals later... just freeze portions flat in plastic zipping bags. Use for stir-fry dishes, to make soups thick & hearty or to mix with fresh vegetables for an easy side dish.

Hearty Red Beans & Rice

Serves 4 to 6

3 slices bacon, crisply cooked
    and crumbled, drippings
    reserved
1 green pepper, chopped
1 onion, chopped
1/2 c. green onion, chopped
1/2 c. celery, chopped
2 T. fresh parsley, chopped
1/2 lb. Polish sausage, sliced

2 15-oz. cans kidney beans,
    drained and rinsed
6-oz. can tomato paste
2-oz. jar chopped pimentos,
    drained
2 T. catsup
1-1/2 t. Worcestershire sauce
1 t. chili powder
3 c. cooked rice

In a skillet over medium heat, sauté green pepper, onions, celery and parsley in reserved drippings until tender. Stir in bacon and remaining ingredients except rice. Reduce heat; cover and simmer for 30 minutes. Serve over cooked rice.

Try serving a meatless main once a week...
it's economical and healthy too. There are lots of tasty
pasta and rice-based dishes to choose from.

Risotto with Asparagus

Serves 3 to 5

2 14-1/2 oz. cans vegetable
    broth
2 T. olive oil
1 c. onion, chopped
1 c. celery, thinly sliced
2 cloves garlic, minced

1-1/2 c. Arborio rice, uncooked
1 lb. asparagus, trimmed and
    cut into 1-1/2 inch pieces
1/3 c. grated Parmesan cheese
1 T. butter, softened

Measure broth; add enough water to make 5-3/4 cups liquid. Bring to
a simmer in a saucepan; reduce heat to low. Heat oil in a large skillet;
add onion, celery and garlic. Sauté for 4 to 5 minutes, until onion is
translucent; add rice and stir for one minute. Add one cup hot broth;
simmer, stirring often, until liquid is almost completely absorbed,
about 4 minutes. Repeat with 2 additional cups hot broth, adding one
cup at a time. Add asparagus and another cup hot broth; cook and
stir until absorbed. Add another cup broth; cook and stir until rice and
asparagus are tender-firm. Remove from heat; stir in cheese, butter
and remaining hot broth. Let stand briefly before serving.

Make a double recipe of your favorite casserole and invite
neighbors over for supper...what a great way to get to know
them better! Keep it simple with a tossed salad, warm bakery
bread and brownies for dessert...it's all about food and fellowship!

48

Pizza Casserole

Serves 16 to 20

2 lbs. ground beef
1 onion, chopped
2 28-oz. jars spaghetti sauce
16-oz. pkg. rotini pasta, cooked

2 8-oz. pkgs. shredded
    mozzarella cheese
8-oz. pkg. sliced pepperoni

In a large skillet over medium heat, brown beef and onion; drain. Stir
in spaghetti sauce and pasta. Transfer to 2 greased, 13"x9" baking
pans. Sprinkle with cheese; top with pepperoni. Bake, uncovered,
at 350 degrees for 25 to 30 minutes.

A crisp green salad goes well with all kinds of hot casseroles.
For a zippy lemon dressing, shake up 1/2 cup olive oil,
1/3 cup lemon juice and one tablespoon of Dijon mustard in
a small jar; chill to blend.

Chicken & Rice Casserole

Serves 8

4 to 5 boneless, skinless chicken breasts, cooked and cubed
6.9-oz. pkg. chicken-flavored rice vermicelli mix, cooked
14-1/2 oz. can French-style green beans
1 c. mayonnaise
8-oz. can sliced water chestnuts, drained
10-3/4 oz. can cream of celery soup
salt and pepper to taste
Garnish: grated Parmesan cheese

Combine ingredients together; place in a greased 13"x9" baking pan. Bake, uncovered, at 350 degrees until golden, about 30 to 45 minutes.

A crunchy topping makes any casserole even tastier. Savory cracker crumbs, crushed tortilla chips or toasted, buttered bread crumbs are all delicious... just sprinkle on before baking.

Dilly Tuna Casserole

Serves 6

1/2 c. mayonnaise
1/2 c. milk
10-3/4 oz. can cream of
    mushroom soup
1 c. shredded Cheddar cheese

1/2 t. dill weed
6-oz. pkg. rotini pasta, cooked
6-oz. can tuna, drained
1 c. potato chips, crushed

Combine mayonnaise and milk; stir in soup, cheese and dill. Gently stir in cooked pasta and tuna. Pour into a lightly greased 1-1/2 quart casserole dish. Cover and bake at 350 degrees for 30 minutes. Uncover and sprinkle with potato chips; bake an additional 5 minutes.

Cream of mushroom, cream of chicken and all the other cream soups blend so well with rice and pasta. Stock up when they go on sale and you'll always be able to whip up a quick & tasty meal.

Beef & Rice Hot Pot

Serves 4 to 6

1 lb. ground beef
1 onion, chopped
2 stalks celery, chopped
salt and pepper to taste
1/2 c. long-cooking brown rice,
    uncooked
1/2 c. long-cooking white rice,
    uncooked

10-3/4 oz. can cream of chicken
    soup
6 T. soy sauce
2-1/2 c. water
Garnish: chow mein noodles

Brown ground beef, onion and celery in a large skillet over medium heat; drain. Add salt and pepper to taste. Stir in remaining ingredients except noodles; bring to a boil. Reduce heat; cover and simmer for 20 minutes, or until liquid is absorbed. Top servings with noodles.

To shred a block of cheese easily, place the wrapped cheese in the freezer for 10 to 20 minutes...it will just glide across the grater!

Country Pasta with Mozzarella

Serves 6 to 8

8 slices bacon, cut into 1-inch
    pieces
2 c. broccoli, chopped
1/2 t. garlic, minced
8-oz. pkg. rigatoni pasta,
    cooked

8-oz. pkg. shredded mozzarella
    cheese
1/4 c. grated Parmesan cheese
1/8 t. cayenne pepper
Garnish: fresh parsley, chopped

Cook bacon in a large skillet over medium heat, stirring occasionally,
until crisp. Add broccoli and garlic; cook until broccoli is crisp-tender.
Drain; stir in rigatoni, mozzarella, Parmesan and cayenne. Heat
through until cheese is melted. Sprinkle with parsley.

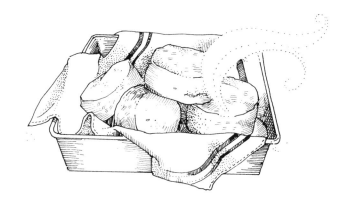

Fluffy hot biscuits are a must with any one-pot meal!
Add a personal touch to refrigerated biscuits...brush with
butter, then sprinkle with dried herbs, coarse salt or
sesame seed before baking.

Woodland Wild Rice

Makes 4 to 8 servings

2 lbs. ground pork country-
  style sausage
1 to 2 sweet onions, sliced
16-oz. pkg. sliced mushrooms

16-oz. pkg. wild rice, uncooked
2 10-3/4 oz. cans cream of
  mushroom soup

Sauté together sausage and onions in a large Dutch oven over
medium heat until browned. Add mushrooms and sauté for 4 to
5 additional minutes. Drain and remove from Dutch oven; set aside.
Cook wild rice in Dutch oven according to package directions until
nearly tender, about 45 minutes. Combine rice with sausage mixture;
fold in soup and mix well. Heat through.

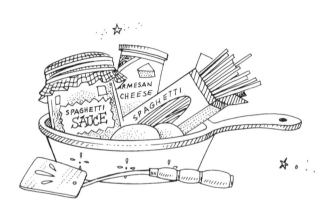

Turn leftover spaghetti into tasty noodle patties. Mix 2 to 3 cups cold, cooked pasta with 2 beaten eggs and 1/2 cup ricotta cheese; form into 4 patties. Cook in a skillet in a little oil until golden. Serve topped with warm spaghetti sauce...yum!

Herbed Zucchini & Pasta

Serves 4

2 T. butter
1/4 c. oil, divided
1 clove garlic, minced
1 onion, chopped
1 green pepper, diced
3 zucchini, halved lengthwise
    and sliced

1 t. dried parsley
1 t. dried rosemary
1 t. dried basil
16-oz. pkg. bowtie or ziti pasta,
    cooked
1/2 c. grated Parmesan cheese

Melt butter with 2 tablespoons oil in a skillet over medium heat; add garlic and onion. Sauté for 5 minutes; stir in green pepper and sauté for an additional 3 minutes. Stir in zucchini and herbs; cook for 5 to 8 minutes, or until zucchini is tender. Add remaining oil; toss with pasta. Sprinkle with Parmesan cheese.

A splash of ginger ale in orange or cranberry juice makes
a refreshing beverage to accompany any casual meal.
Serve in tall glasses with lots of ice.

Shelly's Pork Chops & Rice

Serves 4 to 6

4 to 6 pork chops
1 T. oil
10-3/4 oz. can cream of
    mushroom soup

4-oz. can sliced mushrooms,
    drained and liquid reserved
2 c. long-cooking rice,
    uncooked

Brown pork chops lightly in oil in a skillet over medium heat; drain
and set aside. Combine soup, reserved liquid from mushrooms and
enough water to equal 3 cups; mix well and pour into skillet. Stir in
mushrooms and rice; top with pork chops. Cover and simmer for
30 to 45 minutes, or until rice is tender.

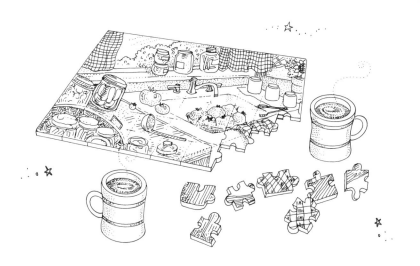

Family night! Serve a simple supper, then spend the evening playing favorite board games or assembling jigsaw puzzles together.

Beef Porcupine Meatballs

Makes 4 to 6 servings

8-oz. pkg. beef-flavored rice
    vermicelli mix, uncooked
    and divided
1 lb. ground beef

1 egg, beaten
2-1/2 c. water
cooked egg noodles

Combine rice vermicelli mix with ground beef and egg, setting aside
seasoning packet from mix. Shape into small meatballs; brown on all
sides in a skillet over medium heat. Drain. Combine contents of
seasoning packet with water; pour over meatballs. Cover and simmer
over low heat for 30 minutes. Serve meatballs and sauce over cooked
egg noodles.

For a healthy change, give whole-wheat pasta a try in your
favorite pasta recipe...it tastes great and contains
more fiber than regular pasta.

Country Noodle Dish

Makes 4 to 6 servings

1 lb. ground beef or turkey
1 onion, chopped
Optional: 2 T. green pepper,
    chopped
11-oz. can corn, drained

2 10-3/4 oz. cans tomato soup
8-oz. pkg. medium egg noodles,
    cooked
1/2 to 3/4 c. water
salt and pepper to taste

In a skillet over medium heat, brown meat with onion and green pepper, if using. Drain; stir in corn. Stir in soup, cooked noodles and water to desired consistency. Add salt and pepper to taste. Heat through and serve.

Spaghetti & meatballs is a delightful, inexpensive main for
a casual get-together with friends. Just add warm garlic bread,
a big tossed salad and plenty of paper napkins!

Good Ol' Spaghetti & Meatballs *Makes 8 servings*

2 14-1/2 oz. cans chunky diced
   tomatoes
2 6-oz. cans tomato paste
2/3 c. water
1 t. Italian seasoning

24 frozen meatballs, thawed
16-oz. pkg. thin spaghetti,
   cooked
Garnish: grated Parmesan
   cheese

Combine tomatoes, tomato paste, water and seasoning in a medium
saucepan. Bring to a boil over medium heat; reduce heat and simmer
for 5 minutes. Add meatballs and heat through. Ladle sauce and
meatballs over cooked spaghetti; sprinkle with cheese.

Church Supper Menu:
- Macaroni Salad
- Baked Beans
- Pretzel Salad

Casseroles that feed a crowd are great take-alongs for any potluck or carry-in. Keep them warm by wrapping the dish in aluminum foil and then tucking it into a newspaper-lined basket.

Chop Suey Casserole

Makes 6 servings

1 lb. ground beef
2 onions, chopped
1 c. celery, chopped
1/4 c. soy sauce
10-3/4 oz. can cream of
    mushroom soup

10-3/4 oz. can cream of chicken
    soup
1-1/2 c. warm water
1/2 c. long-cooking rice,
    uncooked
3-oz. can chow mein noodles

Brown ground beef in a large skillet over medium heat; drain. Stir in onions, celery, soy sauce, soups, water and rice. Transfer to a lightly greased 13"x9" baking pan. Bake, covered, at 350 degrees for 45 minutes. Sprinkle chow mein noodles over top. Return to oven, uncovered, for 15 minutes.

Turn any casserole into an au gratin. Sprinkle an unbaked
casserole with shredded cheese and bread crumbs...a great use
for day-old bread! Blend a little melted butter with dried herbs
and drizzle over the casserole, then bake as usual.

Turkey Tetrazzini

Makes 6 servings

8-oz. pkg. thin spaghetti,
  uncooked
2 cubes chicken bouillon
2 to 3 T. dried, minced onion
2 10-3/4 oz. cans cream of
  mushroom soup
8-oz. container sour cream

1/2 c. milk
salt and pepper to taste
2 c. cooked turkey, cubed
8-oz. can sliced mushrooms,
  drained
8-oz. pkg. shredded Cheddar
  cheese

Cook spaghetti according to package directions, adding bouillon and
onion to cooking water. Drain and place in a large bowl. Stir together
soup, sour cream, milk, salt and pepper in a medium bowl; fold in
turkey and mushrooms. Lightly stir mixture into spaghetti, coating
well. Pour into a lightly greased 13"x9" baking pan; top with cheese.
Bake, uncovered, at 350 degrees for 30 to 40 minutes, until hot
and bubbly.

Visit the farmers' market for the best homegrown veggies...toss a market basket in the car and let the kids pick out fresh flavors for dinner tonight!

Ratatoûille

Serves 6 to 8

1 onion, chopped
3 to 4 cloves garlic, chopped
3 to 4 T. olive oil
2 zucchini, sliced
2 eggplants, peeled and cubed
2 green peppers, sliced

28-oz. can crushed tomatoes
1 t. dried parsley
1 t. dried oregano
1 t. dried basil
4 c. cooked rice

Sauté onion and garlic in olive oil. Add remaining ingredients except rice. Simmer over medium heat for 30 minutes, or until vegetables are tender. Serve over cooked rice.

Herbs and spices add lots of flavor to food, but can be costly
at supermarkets. Instead, purchase them at dollar stores,
bulk food stores and even ethnic stores, where
they can be quite a bargain.

Husband-Pleasin' Dirty Rice

Serves 6 to 8

1 lb. ground beef
1 lb. sage-flavored ground pork
    sausage
1/2 c. onion, chopped

1/2 c. celery, chopped
3 c. water
3 c. instant rice, uncooked

Brown beef, sausage, onion and celery in a skillet over medium heat.
Drain; add water and bring to a boil. Add rice and stir very well.
Remove from heat; cover and let stand for 5 minutes. Stir again
and serve.

Soup is so nice when shared. Thank a friend with a basket of
warm rolls and a pot of steaming homemade soup. What a
welcome surprise on a brisk day!

Comforting Chicken Noodle Soup *Makes 8 servings*

3-1/2 lbs. chicken
4 c. water
3 c. chicken broth
2 onions, divided
4 stalks celery, divided
2 cloves garlic, pressed

1 t. salt
1/4 t. dried tarragon
salt and pepper to taste
1/2 t. dried parsley
8-oz. pkg. thin egg noodles,
    uncooked and divided

Place chicken, water and broth in a large soup pot over medium-high heat. Add one quartered onion, 2 halved stalks celery, garlic, salt and tarragon. Bring to a boil. Reduce heat to low; simmer for 45 minutes, or until chicken is very tender. Strain broth into a large container; discard vegetables. Cool chicken and cut into bite-size pieces; discard skin and bone. Skim broth and return to soup pot. Chop remaining onion and celery; add to pot along with salt, pepper and parsley. Bring to a boil; reduce heat and simmer for 15 minutes. Stir in chicken and half of noodles, reserving remaining noodles for another use. Return to a boil; cook 8 to 10 minutes, until noodles are tender.

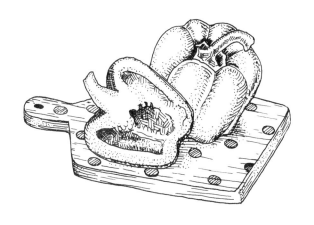

Save the water that vegetables have been cooked in...it makes
a flavorful and nutritious addition to your next pot of soup.

Stuffed Pepper Soup

Serves 8 to 10

2 lbs. ground beef, browned
    and drained
8 c. water
28-oz. can diced tomatoes
28-oz. can tomato sauce
2 c. cooked rice

2 c. green peppers, chopped
2 cubes beef bouillon
1/4 c. brown sugar, packed
2 t. salt
1 t. pepper

Mix together all ingredients in a stockpot; bring to a boil over medium-high heat. Reduce heat and simmer for 30 to 40 minutes, or until green peppers are tender.

Soups are oh-so easy to extend when you need to feed a few more people. Just add a quick-cooking add-in like ramen noodles, orzo pasta or instant rice and simmer for a few more minutes.

Chunky Minestrone

Makes 5 servings

1 T. olive oil
1-1/2 c. onion, chopped
1 carrot, peeled and sliced
2 cloves garlic, minced
14-1/2 oz. can diced tomatoes
4 c. chicken broth
1 c. water
1 t. Italian seasoning

1/2 c. long-cooking rice or soup
    pasta, uncooked
15-oz. can kidney beans,
    drained and rinsed
1 zucchini, chopped
1/2 t. pepper
Garnish: grated Parmesan
    cheese

In a Dutch oven, heat oil over medium heat. Add onion, carrot and garlic; cook for 3 minutes, or until tender. Stir in tomatoes with juice, broth, water, seasoning and uncooked rice or pasta. Bring to a boil. Reduce heat and simmer, uncovered, for 20 minutes, or until rice or pasta is tender. Stir in beans, zucchini and pepper; simmer for 5 minutes. Sprinkle with cheese before serving.

Pack leftover mains or soups into small containers for next day's lunch...you've got a delicious mini meal all set to go.

Cream of Tomato Soup

2 10-3/4 oz. cans tomato soup
4 c. chicken broth
14-1/2 oz. can diced tomatoes
1/2 c. brown or white long-
    cooking rice, uncooked
2 T. olive oil
1-1/2 c. cooked chicken,
    chopped

2 T. dried parsley
1 T. dried basil
2 T. butter
1/4 to 1/3 c. whipping cream
    or half-and-half

Combine all ingredients except butter and cream or half-and-half in
a medium stockpot. Simmer, stirring occasionally, over medium-low
heat for about one hour and 15 minutes. Add butter; stir to melt.
Blend in cream or half-and-half just before serving.

It's the unexpected touches that make the biggest impressions. When serving soup, offer a variety of fun toppings...fill bowls with shredded cheese, oyster crackers, chopped onions and crunchy croutons, then invite everyone to dig in!

Best-Ever Vegetable Soup

Makes 6 servings

2-lb. boneless beef chuck roast
1 onion, chopped
26-oz. can tomato soup
32-oz. pkg. frozen mixed
    vegetables

16-oz. pkg. medium egg
    noodles, uncooked
salt, pepper and nutmeg
    to taste

Place roast in a one-gallon stockpot; add water to cover. Simmer over medium heat until roast is tender, about 1-1/2 to 2 hours. Remove meat, reserving broth. Trim fat from meat and cut into bite-size pieces; return meat to broth. Add onion and return to simmering; stir in remaining ingredients. Simmer an additional 30 minutes, until vegetables and noodles are tender.

Keep an eye open at tag sales for big, old-fashioned enamelware stockpots. They're just right for cooking up family-size portions of soup.

Cheesy Wild Rice Soup

Serves 6 to 8

9 to 10 slices bacon, diced
1 onion, chopped
2 10-3/4 oz. cans cream of
    potato soup

1-1/2 c. cooked wild rice
2 pts. half-and-half
2 c. American cheese, shredded

In a skillet over medium heat, sauté bacon and onion together
until bacon is crisp and onion is tender. Drain and set aside.
Combine soup and rice in a medium saucepan; stir in bacon mixture,
half-and-half and cheese. Cook over low heat until cheese melts,
stirring occasionally.

Homemade savory crackers are a special touch for soup.
Spread saltines with softened butter, then sprinkle with garlic salt,
thyme, paprika or another favorite seasoning. Pop into
a 350-degree oven just until golden, 3 to 6 minutes.

Broccoli-Cheese Soup

Makes 10 to 12 servings

3/4 c. onion, chopped
2 T. oil
6 c. water
6 cubes chicken bouillon
8-oz. pkg. thin egg noodles, uncooked
2 10-oz. pkgs. frozen chopped broccoli

6 c. milk
16-oz. pkg. pasteurized process cheese spread, diced
1 t. salt
1/8 t. pepper
1/8 t. garlic powder

Sauté onion in oil in a skillet over medium heat; drain and set aside. Bring water to a boil in a stockpot; add bouillon, noodles and broccoli. Simmer until tender, about 7 to 10 minutes. Add onion mixture and remaining ingredients; reduce heat. Cover and simmer without boiling, until heated through and cheese is melted.

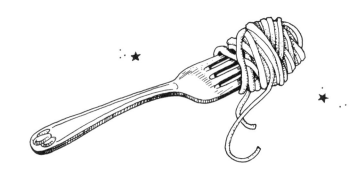

Add some fresh broccoli, asparagus or snow peas to a favorite pasta recipe...simply drop veggies into the pasta pot halfway through the cooking time. Pasta and veggies will be tender at about the same time.

Tomato-Basil Linguine

Makes 8 to 10 servings

4 to 5 tomatoes, coarsely
    chopped
1 lb. Cheddar cheese, diced
1/2 to 3/4 c. olive oil
1/2 t. salt

2 to 4 T. dried basil
4 to 5 cloves garlic, minced
16-oz. pkg. linguine pasta,
    cooked

In a large serving bowl, combine all ingredients except pasta, adding basil and garlic to taste. Let stand at room temperature for 30 minutes to 1-1/2 hours. At serving time, add hot cooked pasta and toss well. Serve immediately.

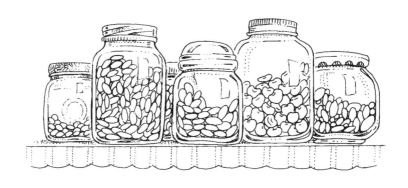

Oversized canning jars make super countertop storage
for pasta and rice.

Foolproof Rice Pilaf

Makes 5 servings

7-oz. pkg. thin spaghetti,
  uncooked and divided
1/4 c. butter

1 c. long-cooking rice, uncooked
3 c. chicken broth
2 to 3 T. sugar

Break up enough spaghetti to measure 1/2 cup; reserve remaining
spaghetti for another recipe. Melt butter in a large saucepan over
medium heat. Add broken spaghetti; cook and stir constantly until
lightly golden. Add rice; cook and stir until blended. Add broth and
sugar to taste. Simmer, covered, over medium heat for 20 to
25 minutes.

An easy chicken bake to serve with Spicy Sesame Noodles.
Place boneless chicken breasts on aluminum foil and drizzle with
soy sauce, sesame oil and lemon juice. Seal packet and bake at
350 degrees about 20 minutes, or until juices run clear.
Add some steamed snow peas...dinner is served!

Spicy Sesame Noodles

Makes 8 to 10 servings

10 c. water
5 3-oz. pkgs. ramen noodles,
    divided
2 cloves garlic
1/2 c. oil

1/4 c. soy sauce
2 t. sesame oil
2 t. red pepper flakes
2 T. sesame seed

Bring water to a boil in a large stockpot. Add noodles (reserving seasoning packets for another recipe) and garlic; boil for 3 minutes. Drain well and discard garlic; mix in remaining ingredients. Serve immediately.

Even a simple family supper can be memorable when it's thoughtfully served. Use the good china, set out cloth napkins and a vase of fresh flowers...after all, who's more special than your family?

Country Brown Rice Dressing

Makes 8 servings

2 c. water
1 c. long-cooking brown rice,
    uncooked
1/4 lb. ground pork or turkey
    sausage
3 c. sliced mushrooms
1 c. onion, chopped

3/4 c. carrot, peeled and
    shredded
1/2 c. sweetened dried
    cranberries
1/4 c. fresh parsley, chopped
2 T. fresh basil, chopped
salt and pepper to taste

Bring water to a boil in a saucepan. Stir in rice; cover and simmer over low heat for 20 to 25 minutes, or until tender. In a large skillet over medium heat, cook sausage, mushrooms and onion until sausage is browned and vegetables are tender. Drain; stir in carrot, cranberries and herbs. Stir cooked rice into sausage mixture; add salt and pepper to taste. Cook and stir until heated through.

Noodles are not only amusing, but delicious.

~Julia Child

Farmhouse Egg Noodles   *Makes 4 to 6 servings*

1 c. all-purpose flour
1 egg, beaten
3 T. milk

1/8 t. salt
3 to 4 14-1/2 oz. cans
    chicken broth

Place flour in a large bowl; make a well in the center and add egg, milk and salt. Slowly stir to mix in flour until a soft ball forms; knead in any remaining flour. Roll out dough on a floured surface to about 1/4-inch thick. Roll up dough jelly-roll style; slice across to cut noodles about 1/2-inch wide. Unroll noodles and pile them on a floured surface while waiting for broth to warm. In a large saucepan, bring broth to a boil. Drop noodles into broth. Cook until tender, about 8 to 10 minutes. Serve noodles in broth or drain and add to a favorite recipe.

Fresh mushrooms of all kinds add earthy flavor to rice and
pasta dishes. When purchasing them, look for smooth
dry caps without cracks. Wash them immediately before
using them but not ahead of time.

Wild Rice & Mushrooms

Serves 10 to 12

10-1/2 oz. can beef consommé
10-1/2 oz. can French onion
    soup
2-1/4 c. water
1/2 c. butter, melted

13-1/4 oz. can sliced
    mushrooms, drained
1 c. wild rice, uncooked
1 c. long-cooking brown rice,
    uncooked

Combine all ingredients in a slow cooker; stir well. Cover and cook on
low setting for 7 to 8 hours, until rice is tender.

Pick up a roast chicken at the deli for 2 easy meals in one. Serve it hot the first night, then slice or cube the rest to become the delicious start of a salad, soup or sandwich supper another night.

Kay's Chinese Chicken Salad

Serves 8 to 10

3-oz. pkg. chicken-flavored
    ramen noodles, uncooked
    and divided
1 head cabbage, shredded
4 boneless, skinless chicken
    breasts, cooked and
    shredded

2 T. onion, chopped
2 T. slivered almonds, toasted
2 T. sesame seed, toasted

Set aside ramen noodle seasoning packet for dressing; crush noodles. Combine all ingredients except seasoning packet in a large serving bowl; toss lightly to combine. Drizzle with dressing and toss again.

Dressing:

1 c. oil
3 T. sugar
1/3 c. vinegar

2 t. salt
reserved ramen noodle
    seasoning packet

Whisk together all ingredients.

Looking for an entertaining idea that's easy on the budget?
Invite family & friends to a potluck! Ask guests to bring a
favorite dish, while you provide plates, napkins and pitchers of
cool beverages. Everyone is sure to have a great time.

San Francisco Salad

Serves 4 to 6

6-oz. jar marinated artichoke
    hearts
4-oz. can sliced black olives,
    drained
2 green onions, chopped

6.9-oz. pkg. chicken-flavored
    rice vermicelli mix, cooked
1/2 c. mayonnaise
1/2 t. curry powder

Drain artichokes, reserving liquid, and chop. Add artichokes, olives
and onions to cooked rice vermicelli mix. In a separate bowl, blend
together mayonnaise, reserved artichoke liquid and curry powder;
stir into rice mixture. Serve warm or chilled.

For hearty salads in a snap, keep cans and jars of diced
tomatoes, black olives and marinated artichokes in the fridge.
They'll be chilled and ready to toss with fresh greens and
cooked rice or pasta at a moment's notice.

Picnic Spaghetti Salad

Serves 6 to 8

8-oz. pkg. spaghetti, uncooked
  and coarsely broken
16-oz. pkg. coleslaw mix
1 onion, chopped

1 green pepper, chopped
1 c. mayonnaise
15-oz. jar coleslaw dressing

Cook spaghetti according to package directions; drain and rinse with cold water. Place in a large serving bowl; add remaining ingredients. Mix well; refrigerate until chilled.

Turn a savory rice side dish into a main in moments...stir in some leftover diced or shredded cooked chicken, beef or pork.

Green Chile Rice Bake

Serves 6

3 c. cooked rice
8-oz. pkg. shredded Monterey
    Jack cheese
1 c. sour cream
7-oz. can diced green chiles

1/4 c. butter, melted
1/2 t. salt
1/2 c. shredded Cheddar cheese
Optional: paprika

Combine all ingredients except Cheddar cheese and paprika in a
greased shallow 2-quart casserole. Top with Cheddar cheese; sprinkle
with paprika, if desired. Bake, uncovered, at 350 degrees for
30 minutes, or until heated through and bubbly around the edges.

Scoop out ripe red tomatoes and fill with
a chilled pasta salad...delicious!

Mediterranean Pasta Salad

Serves 8 to 10

12-oz. pkg. bowtie pasta,
    cooked
12-oz. jar marinated artichoke
    hearts, drained and chopped
2-1/4 oz. can sliced black
    olives, drained

1 cucumber, chopped
1 pt. cherry tomatoes
3 T. sweet onion, chopped
8-oz. bottle balsamic vinaigrette
    salad dressing
6-oz. pkg. crumbled feta cheese

Rinse pasta with cold water; drain well. Toss together all ingredients
except cheese. Refrigerate for 2 to 3 hours. Before serving, toss
with cheese.

Garden-fresh herbs make the best butter. Blend together
1/2 cup butter with 3 tablespoons chopped chives.
Spread over warm rolls or tossed with hot noodles,
this butter is simply delicious!

Savannah Red Rice

1 lb. bacon
1/2 c. onions, chopped
1/2 c. celery, chopped
4 c. stewed tomatoes

2 c. long-cooking rice, uncooked
1/2 t. salt
1/4 t. pepper
1/8 t. hot pepper sauce

In a large skillet over medium heat, cook bacon until crisp. Remove bacon from pan, reserving drippings. Cook onions and celery in drippings until tender; add tomatoes, rice and seasonings. Add crumbled bacon last. Cook over low heat for 10 minutes. Transfer to a greased 3-quart casserole dish and cover tightly. Bake at 350 degrees for one hour, stirring with fork several times.

Turn any casserole into an overnight time-saver. Simply prepare a favorite casserole recipe the night before, cover and refrigerate. Just add 15 to 20 extra minutes to the baking time, until it's hot and bubbly.

Cheesy Spinach Baked Ziti

Serves 4

12-oz. pkg. ziti pasta, cooked
14-1/2 oz. can diced tomatoes
    with Italian herbs
9-oz. pkg. frozen creamed
    spinach, thawed

8-oz. pkg. grated Romano
    cheese
8-oz. pkg. shredded mozzarella
    cheese

Mix all ingredients except mozzarella cheese; spread in a greased
13"x9" baking pan. Top with mozzarella cheese. Cover and bake at
350 degrees for 30 minutes, until hot and bubbly.

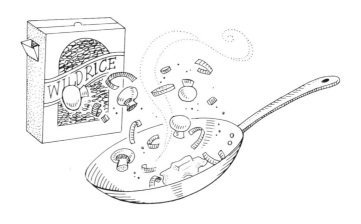

Jazz up a packaged wild rice mix...it's easy. Sauté a cup of chopped mushrooms, onion and celery in butter until tender, then add rice mix and prepare as usual.

Golden Rice Pie

Serves 4 to 6

8-oz. pkg. mushrooms, chopped
1 t. garlic, minced
2 T. olive oil
10-oz. pkg. frozen spinach,
  thawed

2 c. cooked rice
1 c. sour cream
1 c. shredded Swiss cheese
salt and pepper to taste

In a skillet over medium heat, sauté mushrooms and garlic in olive oil; add spinach. Cook until separated; set aside. In a bowl, combine rice, sour cream, cheese, salt and pepper. Spread half of mixture in the bottom of a greased 13"x9" baking pan. Top with mushroom mixture; add remaining rice mixture. Bake, uncovered, at 375 degrees for 45 minutes, or until golden.

For a change of pace, try serving hot cooked rice with butter,
cream and sugar for breakfast. You can even top it
with fresh fruit or a dash of cinnamon.

Caramel Rice Pudding

Makes 8 servings

14-oz. can sweetened
    condensed milk
12-oz. can evaporated milk
1 t. vanilla extract
3 c. cooked rice

1/2 to 2/3 c. sweetened dried
    cranberries
1 T. brown sugar, packed
1 t. cinnamon

In a medium bowl, mix all ingredients except brown sugar and cinnamon. Spoon into a slow cooker that has been sprayed with non-stick vegetable spray. Cover and cook on low setting for 3 to 4 hours, until liquid is absorbed. Before serving, stir pudding; sprinkle with brown sugar and cinnamon. Serve warm.

The discovery of a new dish does more for the happiness
of mankind than the discovery of a star.

~Brillat-Savarin

Apple Kugel

Makes 12 servings

8-oz. pkg. medium egg noodles,
   uncooked
4 T. oil, divided
4 eggs
1/3 c. sugar

1 c. orange juice
1/4 t. cinnamon
1/8 t. ground ginger
1/8 t. salt
1 apple, cored, peeled and diced

Cook noodles according to package directions; drain and toss with
2 tablespoons oil. In a large bowl, mix eggs, sugar, orange juice,
seasonings and remaining oil. Add apples. Combine mixture with
noodles and transfer to a greased 10"x10" baking pan. Cover and
bake at 350 degrees for 40 minutes. Uncover and bake an additional
10 to 20 minutes. Cut into squares.

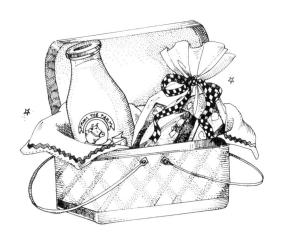

Icy milk served in vintage pint-size milk bottles adds fun to family dessert time and is perfect paired with sweet Butterscotch Haystacks.

Butterscotch Haystacks

Makes 18 servings

2 6-oz. pkgs. butterscotch   1 c. cocktail peanuts
  chips   3-oz. can chow mein noodles

Melt butterscotch chips in a double boiler; stir in peanuts and noodles.
Remove from heat; drop by teaspoonfuls onto wax paper. Set aside
to cool until firm.

INDEX

INDEX

Our Story

Back in 1984, we were next-door neighbors raising our families in the little town of Delaware, Ohio. We were two moms with small children looking for a way to do what we loved and stay home with the kids too. We shared a love of home cooking and making memories with family & friends. After many a conversation over the backyard fence, **Gooseberry Patch** was born.

We put together the first catalog & cookbooks at our kitchen tables and packed boxes from the basement, enlisting the help of our loved ones wherever we could. From that little family, we've grown to include an amazing group of creative folks who love cooking, decorating and creating as much as we do.

Hard to believe it's been over 25 years since those kitchen-table days. Today we're best known for our homestyle, family-friendly cookbooks, now recognized as national bestsellers! We love hand-picking the recipes and are tickled to share our inspiration, ideas and more with you. One thing's for sure, we couldn't have done it without our friends all across the country. Whether you've been along for the ride from the beginning or are just discovering us, welcome to our family!

Want to hear the latest from **Gooseberry Patch**?
www.gooseberrypatch.com

Join Our Circle of Friends

Find us on Facebook

Follow us on twitter

Vickie & JoAnn

1·800·854·6673